Copyright © 2021 Tekkan
Artwork Copyright © 2021

All rights reserved.
First Printing, 2021
ISBN 978-1-7363537-1-4

To contact Tekkan please email:
buddhaboy1289@gmail.com

How to Read My Poems

I have married the sonnet to the tanka. I tell a story in the sonnet — using three quatrains separated by line spaces, and a final couplet. The story builds to a conclusion in the couplet. The tanka is a commentary, or a counterpoint, to the sonnet — the combined poems have two endings.

Recently I have added limericks, doggerel, and rhymed sonnets into my repertoire. The limericks are rhymed but the tanka are not.

I don't usually rhyme my sonnets, because I want freer expression. I want to be direct in my meaning — I want people to clearly understand my meaning. The metaphors are inspired by Shakespeare, and the (aimed-for) precision is in imitation of Japanese style. Using the sonnet with the tanka, I mix the sensibility of the Occident and the Orient — which I have done by living in England, Japan, and America.

I don't punctuate much in my poetry. I want the words themselves to do the work. There is logic between words, and the forms provide structure. By not using punctuation I hope to direct readers to carefully attend to each word — to appreciate the graininess of words.

Reading my poems silently, say, on a bus, a train, or an airplane, and reading them aloud, may be different experiences. The way I've written, there's not always a pause intended at the end of the line.

Hint: *My poems are to be recited not as lines but as phrases, and a phrase often overflows the break at the end of a line. I pause and take a breath where it seems natural for me to pause. Another person may pause differently than I do.*

Each single poem is a piece of a mosaic, and it is my hope that the collection of poems forms an accurate portrait of consciousness.

My daughter, Jocelyn MacDonald, is a wonderful artist. Her artwork graces this book.

I am Barry MacDonald. I received the *dharma* name *Tekkan*, which means "Iron Man," a settled practitioner of great determination.

— *Tekkan*

Everyday Mind XIX

Morning light
spreads
bitter cold
penetrates.

Words
are
incapable
of describing
the wild
gesturing
of
leafless
winter
trees.

The indigo bunting migrates at night
Following stars for orientation
Adjusting the angle guiding its flight
Taking its bearings from constellations
The brilliant bluest blue of all the birds
Its feathers refract and reflect the light
Its beauty far surpasses all my words
Seeing it suddenly is a delight
The birds will return sometime within May
To flit and frolic on the edge of woods
But its image is helping me today
To overcome my frigid winter moods
The birds nest in roadside thickets fields streams
They also resonate in winter dreams.

February snow
minutely sparkles with
the brightest sunlight
but eventually I
get tired of seeing the snow.

I think today is Super Bowl Sunday
And by quickly perusing with Google
I learn the Kansas City Chiefs will play
The Tampa Bay Buccaneers for boodle
Forty years ago I did like football
My team was the Minnesota Vikings
The Purple People Eaters stood so tall
They destroyed the offense with me cheering
The Vikings went to the Super Bowl twice
And I was enamored and excited
But twice they were humbled like little mice
And I was depressed and disappointed
I think sometimes if the Vikings had won
My entire life would have been more fun.

The Vikings lost not
twice but four times at the
Super Bowl and I
was crushed and haven't watched an
hour of football ever since.

Over my everyday underwear I
Put on both the tops and the bottoms of
My long underwear and I slip on a
Pair of warm socks but they are not enough

Then I don my thickest pair of jeans and
A winter fleece that protects my torso
And arms and wraps quite snuggly about my
Neck and I even wrap a scarf around

My neck and then I slip on the knitted
Socks and insert my feet in the bulky
Winter boots and get inside of my down
Jacket and put on a knitted hat that

Covers my ears and put on a Knitted
Hood grab my mittens and go out the door.

Our meeting at Pioneer
Park for an hour on
Monday morning for
conversation is a
crazy extravagance.

It is 93 million miles away
And I know because of modern science
It was orange when at the horizon
But now it is a blazing burning white

The sky is a cloudless and a pale blue
The snow on the ground is starting to shine
Millions of embedded crystals are lit
The more I look the more gleams I'm seeing

I'm 63 years old but now I am
Young because I am not worried about
Anything and the branches of the trees
Are motionless and the land is quiet

All the branches of the trees are crooked
Appearing natural and beautiful.

Even at my desk
at my window
even with thick socks
the bitter cold
is freezing my toes.

The alarm is triggered at 5 a.m.
And the jingle is quite inoffensive
In fact if I were to choose a tune to
Fall asleep with this would be the warble

And to turn the alarm off I have to
Press upon four squares in numerical
Order on my tablet and to do that
I have to commit to waking up to

Experience the wrenching transition
From a dream of wild adventure or of
Adoration where I was the center
Of heavenly attention back to dull

Reality wherein I have to choose
Whether to get up or return to sleep.

I start my days
groggy
doleful and
disgruntled.

The overhang between sleep and daytime
Awareness is often not such a stark
Transition for me when I find myself
Awake an hour or several hours

Before the dawn when I discover that
Thoughts will run away with my consciousness
When I would much rather be asleep but
Instead I am dwelling on arguments

Or broken relationships or vanished
Opportunities and I have chosen
Sometimes to be a captive of my thoughts
And sometimes I will turn to spiritual

Jujitsu when I rise and assume the
Lotus posture for some meditation.

A simple posture
of the body
positions me
to dissipate
unwanted thoughts.

I would very much like to meet the guy
Who is acting as me inside of my
Dreams as he is the sort of person who
Stands calmly upon the dizzy top of

An alpine mountain in a wingsuit and
Jumps enabling me to imagine
Flying in and out of gargantuan
Alpine shadows and I am having fun

Teasing and taunting Kitcat every day
But he cracks a bullwhip and challenges
Lions and tigers inside of a cage
And the most dangerous activity

I do is driving on the highway but
Volcanoes are in his vicinity.

I would trade
my tranquility
for his
vulnerability
in a heartbeat.

The adventurous fellow in my dreams
Is my avatar weaving symbolic
Subconscious and nightly commentary
Perhaps as dramatic counterpoise to

My ordinary existence and his
Emotions are intense as he loves more
Vividly and gets more terrified than
I do but I suspect my wakeful self

Is much more meditative as I'm not
A whirl of activity and it is
Not so easy to identify which
Of my emotions I am feeling

As I feel emotions differently
As anger resonates along my spine.

I sleep with my
left ear on the pillow
and my left ear
gets plugged
with wax.

The same trees are gesturing outside of
My window every day and if I'm not
Careful if I am busy with the news
Entangling myself with loathing and with

Disgust then the obvious winter trees
Immersed within their dormancy become
Invisible and meaningless to me
But I may return to my body and

Attend to breathing lungs and a beating
Heart and gaze at the unsymmetrical
Brilliance of the crooked and the twisting
Quality of winter trees beyond my

Comprehension as there isn't any
Pattern or design to grasp ahold of.

The leafless trees
exhibit a wild
explosion of
creative
genius.

Imagine if time were variable
And thus you could see within a minute
A tree sprouting and spurting upward from
The ground observing the wiggling and the

Sudden shocking sideways outthrusting of
Its limbs splaying out in its dozens of
Unpredictable directions in an
Explosion of growth and then the finest

And minutest details of the twigs would
Emerge like capillaries all for the
Aiming of individual leaves for
The tasting and absorption of sunlight

As the trees appearing in winter are
A testament to creativity.

Something about
sunlight and soil
prompts the crooked
twisting of
trees.

But such an instantaneous insight
Of an explosive growth of a tree would
Be an injustice to the solicitous
And tenuous exploration of air

On the part of the tree as one wonders
What does the sunlight do to earth and soil
To engender such creativity
As the open sky is revealed to be

A progenitor with the sun and the
Universe and the thing that went bang that
Impelled the cosmos eventually
To arrive at a point where a person

Contemplates just so much interweaving
Of a crazy phantasmagoria.

I am saturated
with the
identical
impetus of
creativity.

I'm back in Pioneer Park on Friday
Temperature minus thirteen degrees
Fahrenheit wrapped inside of layers of
Clothing like an eggroll exuberant

With the extravagance of biweekly
Camaraderie and conversation
With only my cheeks and nose exposed to
The cold as we talk about the joys of

Living without alcohol as the sun
Is cresting the horizon and we are
Discussing who we have harmed and how we
Intend to make amends for the damage

Because that is what we desire to do
To free ourselves from the burden of guilt.

The wide river valley
stretches southward
and a crow's caw
reverberates.

When I have the luxury of being
Free of the compulsion of having to
Do some necessary chore so that it
Is possible to lounge and look out of

The window and watch the drama of the
Clouds and the flights of birds each peculiar
To their species then I often note the
Quiet presence of the trees and I love

To mix their unsymmetrical beauty
With the sensation of my beating heart
The throbbing of blood in my veins and the
Rhythmic pattern of my breathing with the

Awareness that the vibrations of my
Body are interwoven with the earth.

Accumulating snow
fresh snow
bitter cold
make for
a meditative
trance.

The sky isn't completely covered with
Clouds as wind-shredded openings appear
But the clouds are dominating the sky
At the moment and I find it pleasant

To remind myself that even when the
Sun isn't visible the clouds glow white
Because of the eminence of the sun
And I can close my eyes while facing the

Window on a bitter cold day and my
Eyelids are red and also infused with
Penetrating sunlight and I also
Sense the pulsation of my eyes and of

My whole body as if the sun itself
Were the vibrating and pulsating source.

The burning of the sun
and the pulsation
of my body are
simpatico.

The concatenation of the human world
Crazed bickering insatiable
Is on parade in the news media
And it's helpful to take a holiday

From the disturbing issues as long as
Someone doesn't come along to take
A bite out of me or of someone whom
I love wherein there is my dilemma

That I do need to follow the drift of
Society but it's beneficial
To lounge and return to the beating of
My heart and the breathing of my lungs and

The wind has swept the clouds from the sky
And the shadows of trees lie on fresh snow.

Fresh gleaming snow
A million pinpoint jewels
of red green blue
are permutations of
a burning sun.

I am pondering whether the beating
Of my heart and the pulsation of my
Body are more than simpatico with
The eminence of the sun and whether

The sun itself is burning vibrating
And pulsating perhaps not in rhythmic
Harmony with human or animal
Hearts but on a different frequency

With the sun imposing its dominance
Rippling warming heating scorching with the
Winter trees responding gradually
In a rhythm of dormancy and of

Leafy vibrancy and whether the whole
Earth is a dance of waving particles.

When I close my eyelids
and sense pulsation
am I only sensing
my body and not
the sun?

Humans manipulate the vibration
Of sounds with violins cellos harps and
Mighty church organs and I can almost
Imagine seeing the vibrant rippling of

Sound impacting in the air as the earth
Exhibits its own tuneful resonance
For instance the return of breezes in
Springtime leaves with voices both profoundly

Joyful or mournful depending upon
My mood and there are innumerable
Continuing reverberations as
For example earlier this morning

The sky was overcome with smothering
Clouds but blusters have swept the clouds away.

Igneous
metamorphic
sedimentary rocks
are a rhythm
of earthly becoming.

The Northern Cardinal doesn't migrate
It fluffs its feathers and endures the cold
In February its calls will vibrate
As the mating of the male becomes bold
Fluttering swooping gliding it appears
A scarlet flash amid the pristine snow
A loveliness of red and white cohere
In an instant a marvelous tableau
A cardinal in winter is a gift
In the middle of a frigid season
Hungry and scavenging it must persist
It is beautiful without a reason
It's exceedingly odd the way things are
That such beauty exists is quite bizarre.

Latent energy
lies dormant inside of the
gnarly contorted
branches of a winter tree
as a cardinal perches.

My head is exhausted so I'm quitting
Scrounging for words is a dreary business
Working so hard while stoically sitting
Fussing with syllables is an illness
Attempting to rhyme contorts the grammar
Very often the meaning makes no sense
Pounding out rhymes with a ball peen hammer
Waiting for ideas creates suspense
I've had too much coffee now I'm weary
My acuity is out the window
I really do want to take it easy
All I can do now is mumbo-jumbo
I am very tired and it's time to quit
Don't especially care if words don't fit.

It is such a waste of time
Straining and trying to rhyme
They're kind of a crutch
They don't mean much
And the poems aren't worth a dime.

Lily the calico cat comes downstairs
To greet me with a grumpy yowling that
Is her way of saying hello after
I get to my desk and window in the

Morning and perhaps her intention is
No more than to expostulate "look at
Me here I am again" — so I yowl with
A rising questioning inflection or

I remark "what do you want?" in people
Language and if she's close enough I will
Grab her and put her on the desk where she
Takes dainty steps upon the scattered sheets

Of paper while jabbering or she may
Sit looking out the window like I do.

Some of us are
irascible within
contented
satisfaction.

With flutters the Black-capped chickadees come
To the feeder in the cold with sideways
Glimpses at each other pecking at the
Seed watching puffing feathers snatching the

Wire mesh with their feet with one asserting
Dominance with one forced to fly away
As the two remaining chickadees hop
Around the feeder out of the windward

And snowy side of the feeder as they
Peck into the feeder and the two seem
To get along until an imposing
Tufted titmouse arrives on scene and

The chickadees are rousted and flee the
Feeder leaving the titmouse to his meal.

Dominance
is asserted
and established
instantaneously.

Lily the cat and my Mom are upstairs
When I arrive at the office which is
Inside of the house wherein I was raised
And I love my resonant solitude

Where the hum of the electricity
From the ancient freezer and the printer
And the bubbling of the aquarium
Engenders vibrations conducive for

Meditative writing with the words and
Phrases coalescing into meaning
Inspiring effervescence but then
Inevitably I hear the sound of

Descending footsteps portending a jolt
Disappointing me with interruption.

Impending
interruption
curdles into
a sour
sigh.

Sometimes I remember my old mentor
Cid Corman pronouncing that rhyme is dead
It's antiquated and lost its vigor
It's much better to speak freely instead
As language isn't so artificial
And resists being tied with pretty bows
The meaning with rhymes is superficial
Poetry becomes vainglorious pose
And rhyming sounds like pontification
The consequence of a fragile ego
It's better to go for self-negation
To exhibit oneself incognito
But is rhyme really dead — maybe not yet
I guess it all depends on a mindset.

It's not very hard to rhyme
And it doesn't take much time
Just type in a word
At RhymeZone.com
And find a rhyme anytime.

Our society is having a purge
Of the menace White Supremacy
So that justice will finally emerge
We have a problem with our history
Because we honor mendacious people
We must destroy statues and monuments
To create a benevolent sequel
The downtrodden will gain predominance
White women are not deserving of blame
But the white Christian men are the problem
We must make propitious use of shame
And follow the path of Joseph Stalin
Historical white men must disappear
And it's time to cancel William Shakespeare.

Shakespeare is just a big dope
Let's get ahold of a rope
We'll circle his head
So he can drop dead
And we can inspire hope.

In their wild beauty standing quietly
On this winter morning I am probing
For what do the trees mean to me today
As I see them through the periphery

Of the window as the rectangular
Window is a man-made fabrication
Worthy of appreciation but the
Naked trees upthrusting skyward are a

Testament of a cosmic genius as
All of the innumerable twigs are
Such delicate fingers and every bud
And leaf to come are eager tongues tasting

Absorbing the pulsation of the sun
Akin to my pulsating beating heart.

Asymmetrical trees
are equivalent in
creative force to
volcanoes.

The snow is descending in the finest
Of grains and I can imagine them to
Be like subatomic particles waving
Within a vast incomprehensible

Ocean of emanation shoreless and
Ceaseless and I recognize myself as
A node of consciousness capable of
Possessing only a glimpse of the truth

As I did nothing to deserve my heartbeat
My mobile body and my sensations
Of exploration and too often I
Am liable to squabble and jab at

Fellow human beings forgetful of
The redemption of curiosity.

I am curious
enough to grow
roots and probe
the sky with
questions.

The trees are dormant during the winter
But that doesn't mean they stand idly by
As roots are keeping them firmly in place
And they resonate mournfully with the

Wind and the blustery winter wind is
Sharp and stimulating so much better
Than the eternal silence of the moon
And I am grateful for the presence of

The trees for the shadows they lay upon
Fresh fallen snow and for the shelter they
Afford the crows chickadees cardinals
And the nuthatches as the winter birds

Are simpatico with the barren trees
Fitting together like yang beside ying.

Without meditative
awareness the trees
remain
invisible.

While waiting for a train in Amsterdam
On the ferry of the English Channel
Thinking about his poems on a tram
Visiting his gravesite in a chapel
I appreciated Shakespeare's sonnets
And adored his Elizabethan pomp
He was quite lovesick and I believed it
Inspiring an ethereal whomp
His verbiage is like thick molasses
With clever rhymes and opal metaphors
He gave vent to superlative passions
Not getting enough and wanting much more
Each of Shakespeare's sonnets is a puzzle
Lyrical exorbitant and subtle.

But I don't know why
anyone would rhyme like that
it's kind of crazy
this Houdini trick with words
is just piffle for the birds.

Sitting facing the window
Quiet like at a Zendo
A cardinal came
Smacked into the pane
And all I could say was "Oh!"

I am not a birder but do enjoy
Pointers passed on to me by Fran saying
Among winter birds in Minnesota
Are the smaller redpolls and house finches

That have similar streaky brown or gray
Markings over their white bellies and backs
And the males of the finches have splashes
Of red about their upper breast and the

Males of redpolls have pink-washed chests with a
Blotch of scarlet on their foreheads and I
Appreciate Fran's knowledge because I've
Never knowingly seen such birds and now

Because of Fran I am an older dog
With an epiphany ahead of me.

In every season
I have faith
there is a
revelation
to watch for.

Out of an empty sky the cardinal
Flew directly toward me and its motion
Instantaneously captivated
My attention and with a fleeting glimpse

I recognized the scarlet bird before
The disconcerting impact against the
Windowpane and he took the blow along
With my breath and flew off to the right

Which discombobulated my hunt for
Rhymes and I've done it also and I
Have walloped my head repeatedly and
There was a winter evening with an

Innocent stroll to a birthday party when
I smashed into and rattled a closed glass door.

I don't know about
the cardinal but for
me embarrassment
is worse than
shock.

Upon exiting my house and locking
The door I notice the caw of a crow
And look about for the bird toward the
Gigantic cottonwood on the corner

Of my property and I see the tree
Coated in a hoar frost and search and spot
The crow perching and I utter a "caw"
In turn and then another crow streaks in

The air to my right seizing my sight for
A moment and not dawdling I go in
The garage heave up the door drive out and
Get out of the car close the garage door

And perhaps another crow or the same
Crow flies by establishing his presence.

The six or seven
crows of the
neighborhood
seem to
recognize me.

By 1903 no one had done it
And I am old enough to remember
The jerky grainy black-and-white films of
Flailing flying contraptions as they launched

Off of piers and crashed into the water
Which I suppose is a propitious
Method for crashing without getting hurt
But the Wright Brothers accomplished the feat

Solving the problems of pitch roll and yaw
Engineering a motor with rotors
An elevator a rudder a right
Warp and curvature for a pair of wings

And at Kitty Hawk North Carolina
People did become flying animals.

It took modern nylon
and a lot more courage
to perfect
wingsuits.

In 2021 the latest
In a series of land rovers made it
To Mars arriving after rocketing
From Earth and traveling a distance of

292 million miles and
The appropriate name of the rover
Is "Perseverance" and this installment
Is unique in deploying over the

Martian surface the aptly entitled
"Ingenuity Helicopter" to
Preview the arid ground that the rover
Will encounter which is a tricky feat

Because the thin Martian atmosphere is
Only one percent of the Earth's air.

It's a challenge
to create enough
lift in the
unbreathable
Martian air.

The bone-chilling temperature on Mars
Is minus one hundred thirty degrees
Fahrenheit and it's a desert without
Oxygen and nothing is alive there

Yet very intelligent people are
Looking to colonize Mars after
Mankind has rendered Earth unlivable
Which is a queer eccentric opinion

Revealing exorbitant hubris
Concerning human capability
But also poisonous cynicism
About embryonic humanity

Because redemption is possible and
Our homely earth is all-encompassing.

How odd that
people can be
so clever
and stupid too.

While adoring the frozen winter trees
Absorbing their wild gesticulations
Appreciating the variety
And the delicacy of winter birds

It's easy to see their interwoven
Compatibility and it's fitting
To be happy about whatever it
Was that exploded 14 billion years

Ago and how marvelous it is to
Be awake and be attentive to the
Ongoing phantasmagoria of
Creation and I need as much of my

Intellect as I can muster but most
Of my adoration comes from my heart.

Who knows what
will emanate
from the
continuing
Big Bang?

I've taken to dangling a stone on a
Chain in front of my chakras to explore
What kind of energy my body is
Emanating at the moment and if

The stone goes around in clockwise circles
Then there's confirmation of a healthy
Equanimity of emotions and
Intellect but if the stone is hanging

Motionless there is evidence of a
Disturbance of the mind and the body
And then I hunt for the bodily source
And I'm finding that fear feels like a mass

Of concrete in my stomach and then it's
Good to consider what's causing the fear.

Thought
triggers
emotion
triggers
emanation.

I have been educated to know that
Every living being gives off subtle
Vibrations of energy even the
Happy woolly bear caterpillars that

Wiggle on the pavement before winter
And next year I will certainly dangle
A stone over them to see how they do
But anytime inside my home I may

Investigate the pitch and humming of
Kitcat only it's necessary to
Catch him unawares otherwise he will
Flip instantly onto his back and swipe

Lunge and bite the stone and then of course it
Is impossible to get a reading.

Kitcat is
always a
ragamuffin
rapscallion.

The amount of snow overnight was more
Than shovel work and it's better not to
Leave the snow blowers idle for too long
So I ran the machines and found the snow

Fluffy on top and greasy beneath and
It was an easy but messy chore in
Later February which signals that
Perhaps the coldest days of winter are

Over as we enter the pattern of
Thawing of snow during daylight and of
Freezing overnight as the trudge through the
Tundra of winter is lifting at last

And soon the brown grass will appear again
As the sunlight regains its potency.

Warming days
lull and tranquilize
but sloppy blizzards
are coming.

I saw outside of my window a pair
Of little gray birds with yellow beaks that
Hopped in the hedge before departing and
Several crows are flying together now

Above the trees and I'm remembering
A Buddhist saying about the empty
Space between things — the emptiness that binds
Everything together without a seam

Is the clarified mind without a thought
Like a mirror that of itself has no
Image contained within it but it does
Reflect all manifested liveliness

As everything I perceive does arise
Outside of and inside of my noggin.

I can't loiter
in clarity
because
the mind
cogitates.

There are things to do in a sudden thaw
Without a smidgeon of hesitation
It's like an ecclesiastical law
And to waste time is a violation
I race to the carwash and wait in line
Because the car is badly encrusted
As the snowplows spew a god-awful brine
And I refuse to let the car be rusted
So I will loiter with the radio
Snug like a bug in a rug in my car
Savoring the frothy sudsy gizmo
And afterward I can grin like a rock star
As life is so brief I do need to act
And enjoy more than my digestive tract.

I patiently wait my turn
Past the point of no return
I can't move an inch
I'm starting to itch
My heart's beginning to burn.

The blanket of snow won't be here for long
It's covered in rabbit and squirrel prints
As much milder days are coming along
But now there are innumerable glints
With sunlight sparking millions of crystals
Their fire is refracting in pinpoint jewels
Becoming sharp iridescent pixels
But quickly this snow will melt into pools
Clouds are making a high thin ceiling
Moving gradually within the sky
But even with the clouds it's revealing
The potency of light will multiply
Spring is approaching and the snow will go
And I will warm myself — like a tomato.

The red squirrel is busy
Running on top of the fence
He stops and he runs
He runs and he stops
Making perfect squirrel sense.

I do admit it isn't really fair
To compare my poems with what they did
It is easy now because of software
While they depended so much upon id
When weary I turn to a thesaurus
When rhyming I go to RhymeZone.com
To find a partner with "polymorphous"
And thereby poetizing with aplomb
But old-time poets relied on their heads
They couldn't surf the web for verbiage
They exhausted their gray matter instead
And they must have mustered so much courage
But I don't care and I am quite happy
That I can rhyme and make it sound snappy.

I come to my desk and sit
Hunting for a rhyme that fits
It's not for acclaim
It's only a game
Choosing a "banana split."

I do like my experiments with rhyme
It's not difficult and just takes practice
But I won't be doing it all of the time
To make it a habit would be madness
It's kind of crazy and not normal speech
It could easily be illogical
To rhyme formally is to sort of preach
And perhaps it is pathological
But just for a lark I would love to see
The president give special emphasis
And concoct a brand-new style by maybe
Rhyming the State of the Union Address
I would love to see that bunch of dummies
Sit and listen as it would be funny.

The president is stoic
He lives by the Potomac
Better than normal
Because he's formal
The president's heroic.

Rhyming is a Houdini trick with words
And there are combinations of words and
Thoughts that would never coalesce without
The impetus of making a rhyme and

I've discovered it is propitious
And wickedly decorous and pithy
To be slyly sarcastic while rhyming
Because creating a tune comports with

Humor but to rhyme and be sincere is
Tricky because in America now
Such formalized poetizing sounds quite
Odd and old-fashioned so striking the right

Tone becomes difficult within a form
That doesn't accommodate wiggle room.

Do you suppose
Pythagoras
could have
impressed by
rhyming
theorems?

You know Thag
It's all very fine
Your theorems
May be perfectly
Accurate
But they don't even rhyme!

I don't operate in isolation
As every action I take will spur a
Reaction as lately there's no problem
For me to fall asleep easily but

When I wake at 2 a.m. and am not
Depressed but my mind is buzzing with a
Self-satisfied happiness which isn't
Conducive for getting back to sleep I

Will spread my cushions upon the floor for
40 minutes of Zen meditation
But Kitcat expects that I am getting
Up and happy brushing time is coming

So he gallops noisily through all the
Rooms in the house and then he caterwauls.

I am seeking
disembodied repose
while Kitcat expects
brushing wrestling
slapping and biting.

I slip seamlessly from a vivid and
Poignant separation from my daughter
In a dream to wakefulness in bed and
I remember my son is living in

Alaska and we habitually
Don't communicate as I notice the
Pulsing of my heartbeat is prompting a
Throbbing sensation within my ears which

Reminds me of my intention to seek
For the locus of emotion within
My body and I think but am not sure
That sadness and grief are felt about my

Stomach as my stomach feels like a chunk
Of concrete which is a load to carry.

Every event of life
even the transition
from a dream is a
seamless continuous
reverberation.

This is an odd season of transition
From bitter cold to thawing and freezing
Overnight and on sunny days water
Will be running across the hilly streets

Of Stillwater down to the wide river
And every year I feel a lifting of
Burdens and a lightening of spirit
Very much like a liberation from

Despair but I have to remind myself
Of my locus in Minnesota where
The snow may melt precipitously to
Reveal the grass on the verging of a

Resurrection but within minutes the
Sky will change and dump a load of snow.

I steel myself
remembering from
November to April
every day is
February.

Around the trunks of my trees in my yard
The thawing of snow is expanding in
Wide circles revealing the brownish grass
And this pattern is repeated throughout

The neighborhood as if the roots of trees
Were warming the earth and melting the snow
Whereas the ground without roots beneath is
Covered in minutely pockmarked snow that

Bears evidence of thawing and freezing
And the wind has been blustery for the
Last few days causing the wild gesturing
Of the bare branches to violently

Sway in the air and I wonder whether
The trees are waking from winter slumber.

There is a new sparkle
in the morning sun
and its corona is
incandescent.

Each sheet of paper that bears evidence
Of my cogitation within the form of
My poetry that you are turning with
Your fingertips every single page that

Falls one upon another as you read
Expresses in the agreed upon forms
Of letters communicates with words and
Lines from me to you all of these pages

Originated in the liveliness
Of the trees the earth and the sun and the
Mixture of the earth air fire and water
Forming a mode of community through

Writing and reading transpiring through
Millennia of civilization.

All the permutations of
emotive
intellection
metamorphize on
wood pulp.

We were born and grew from the earth as a
Permutation of evolution and
Depended upon an interweaving
Of forces including the striking of

The earth by an asteroid prompting the
Extinction of the dinosaurs that made
Possible different forms of being
And the panorama of liveliness

Metamorphizes continually
Encompassing the fearsome certainty
Of other cataclysmic events and
We humans ourselves may even be the

Perpetrators — and even if we were
Would that fact be contrary to nature?

Nature is
incomprehensible
unpredictable
continuous
Wild.

Some of our befuddled scientists are
Supposing that within black holes that
Are scattered throughout the cosmos — and there
Maybe millions inside our Milky Way

Galaxy — there are singularities
Of infinite gravity where time is
Instantaneous and not linear
And the boundary between progressing

And extraordinary time shifts at the
Event horizon drawing everything
Inward with irresistible force and
What possible inference can be drawn

From the dawning of our comprehending
Consciousness of this arrangement of things?

I was nothing before
I became something
and will become nothing
again.

Questions for me percolate surrounding
The quantity and the quality of
Consciousness fixating upon whether
A protozoa has detectable

Selective aliveness and if so what would
Its experience be like and suppose
Assumed inanimate objects like the
Winter trees in Minnesota have an

Original form of thought about them
Responding to shifting temperature
And the orbital proximity of
The sun and if so then the vibrations

Blinking into and out of existence
Of waving quarks are infused with knowledge.

Things blink into and
out of existence from
nothing to something
to nothing.

The air is just about freezing and the
Precipitation is more of snow than
Sleet and the flakes are blowing sideway in
A vigorous wind and I can see the

Hedges and branches of trees are getting
Coated with the sticky kind of snow and
At times like this I wonder where do the
Delicate birds like the chickadee and

The titmouse go and what do they do for
Shelter as the crows and the gulls have more
Substance on their bones to handle this kind
Of moist and penetrating cold but the

Little birds are only skin feathers and
Bone and February can be nasty.

I imagine there are
the sides of hills and
walls or boulders
out of the way of
the blowing snow.

How does one reconcile with conflicting
Views of nature as the animals are
Gifted with claws and teeth and end up
Inside of each other's stomachs and we

Aren't much different with our warfare
Oppression and politics which devolve
Into all the subtle arts of deceit
And gossip and we apply our forms of

Industrial butcheries to species
Of animals for consumption and yet
We have a sensibility that points
To redemption-creating myths serving

To ennoble our perplexing struggles
Turning on courage and benevolence.

Is the warrior's
wrath both
bloody and
innocent?

Seeing the trees sway within a white sky
As the snow is curling sideways down with
A density that partly obscures the
Trees in the distance as the sky and snow

Are inseparable as the sky has
Descended to engulf within itself
All the moving trees of the neighborhood
As I am sheltered within an office and

Am observing warm and dry at my desk
And window typing words of description
Onto a broad computer screen of the
Same shade of white as the sky and snow and

The flakes of snow have become enormous
And every flake must be a touch of cold.

In the near distance I hear
the heavy metal blades
of snowplows scraping
snow off of the asphalt.

I can only see the barest outlines
Of winter trees within the blowing snow
But in fantasy I take possession
Of omnipotent vision instantly

Arriving upon any vantage of
Choosing and I would watch the crest of dawn
Spreading sunlight on the rotating Earth
And next I would take the best view of the

Swirling gaseous red spot of Jupiter
And then I would become a microscope
To observe the revolutions of the
Electrons of atoms and then I would

Launch myself to the edge of the cosmos
To know what is it expanding into.

Perhaps
motion
and
existence
are
inseparable.

According to the weather app on my
Cell phone the snow is supposed to stop in
45 minutes but I am looking
Out of the window now to verify

The cessation of snow and there high in
A tree a crow is perching and just now
I'm seeing another bird perhaps a
Sparrow flit and glide into the maple

And I don't know how the birds operate
But they have left shelter to do business
And I will take my cues from them and zip
Myself inside of a down jacket while

Wearing my big boots preparing to move
This sticky sloppy snow off the driveways.

Doing poetry first
and mindless
activity afterward
is harmonious.

Rhyming sonnets is an amusing game
As long as I admit they don't mean much
It's fun and maybe just a little lame
Even as the habit could be a crutch
Finding blustery words is a puzzle
Striking a pretentious poetic pose
Stirring up drama tempo and sizzle
And finishing with effortless repose
Surely the poet has sincerity
There's no purpose to writing otherwise
Just a useless verbal dexterity
But sometimes it's good to spring a surprise
I could put this sonnet on my tombstone
To inspire a laugh and not a moan.

Here lies Barry cold and dead
Without a thought in his head
He found clarity
And hilarity
With not a word left unsaid.

Snow will be melting in the next two weeks
All the walkways and roads will be a mess
And overnight so much water will freeze
So I walk with more than a little stress
As thin ice is almost invisible
So it's important to be clearheaded
Spotting a glint of ice is pivotal
Because I am not very hardheaded
And don't want to give my noggin a whack
It takes an instant of inattention
And more than my head could suffer a crack
I dread the tears of hyperextension
There are many perils that come with spring
And I don't want to see my legs upswing.

A moment's inattention
Means discombobulation
Involving a whack
Of a hard impact
And then incomprehension.

I am not deceived by appearances
I know all the snow is on the way out
But I don't forget my old grievances
I know what "spring melt" is really about
It is fabulous within a few days
Winter's accumulated snow will go
As the sun is marvelously ablaze
And the grass may even begin to grow
But it's a deception I've seen before
It seems the blizzards are finally gone
I don't have to wear big boots anymore
But it's a trick and I'm not a moron
It's a certainty in Minnesota
April blizzards are part of a quota.

The warmth is all very fine
And I enjoy the sunshine
It's no time for fun
Because we're not done
It will snow multiple times.

In the twilight zone between the ending
Of a dream and waking awareness I
Catch myself or maybe it is better
To say the apparition of ego

Is exposed in a poignant longing for
Things to be different than they are and
I see that the me who desires and
Is repulsed in dreams is identical

With the me of daylight activity
Except within dreams there is a freedom
From mundane circumstances giving space
For fantasy to play but at bottom

I realize I'm having a lot of
Fun wrestling with dissatisfaction.

I'd like to be more
explicit about
the details of the
dream but they slipped by
beyond my grasping.

I arrived home from the office to see
A pair of bald eagles in the branches
Of my cottonwood and as I approached
To get a better look one raised its wings

And it lifted off so impressing me
With the magnitude of its weight and size
In the slowness of its motion that I
Have never seen so close to home and

The neighbor said the excited crows of
The homely neighborhood grew quite upset
At being displaced from the prominence
Of the towering cottonwood by the

Unexpected presence of royalty
Based on superior size and talons.

Kitcat
in the house
won't meet
the eagle's
talons.

Writing sonnets loosey-goosey without
The task of rhyming is much easier
But in the play of rhyming the ends of
The lines I'm finding it's propitious

To be facetious and strike dramatic
Poetical poses variously
Smug or indignant as the poem turns
Which isn't a true personality

But piffle harmonious with rhyming
As I can't fathom being serious
And rhyming too because that would feel like
Wearing a colonial powdered wig

Which might have been OK for John Keats or
Robert Frost but seems obsolete to me.

But be alert
I also strike
piffling poetical poses
without rhyming.

In politics it is easy to lose
There is an art in prevaricating
It is beneficial to skew the news
So many events are irritating
The politicos know how to accuse
Shaping the narrative is important
It is a trick to confuse and abuse
Being honorable is impotent
To rise in the ranks they follow their cues
The system becomes a nasty machine
Originality they won't excuse
The exercise of force is often mean
Most Americans haven't got a clue
They are being deceived — I wish they knew.

He is honest he is bold
His virtue will not be sold
His integrity
And sincerity
Are a beauty to behold.

Give me the company of desperate
Drunks who are struggling to be sober
To drink is to die and they accept it
The forgetful bliss they had is over
The chaos they create is dangerous
They grieve their families and they know it
And then driving while drunk is treacherous
They have compulsion and can't control it
They need to talk to the people like them
They are confused and need to express it
They are terrified of the days to come
The urge is tempting but they repress it
And their loneliness is hard to fathom
It's necessary to hit rock bottom.

An alcoholic
has no control over how
much he drinks once he
starts again and no control
over the consequences.

The scorn he gets is understandable
There is not an easy explanation
The damage is incomprehensible
Apologies prompt exasperation
And the alcoholic is pathetic
Why on earth he can't stop is the question
And quite often he seems apathetic
He's not even open to suggestions
Or he's mournful and apologetic
And expresses the best of intentions
But it is hard to be sympathetic
He's not a person who learns his lessons
His drunken antics are deplorable
Living with him becomes unbearable.

He doesn't know why
he does what he does — even
the hangovers are
not enough to curtail an
inevitable binge.

So how does one help an alcoholic?
Relinquishing control is the first step
Repeating behavior is neurotic
And making excuses is a misstep
He has to hit bottom to get better
He has to suffer the consequences
The more pain he feels — so much the better
He needs to be stripped of his defenses
Coddling or soothing doesn't help him
Keep him from driving when drunk if you can
Call the police and let them arrest him
Let him suffer more pain than he can stand
His hitting rock bottom is essential
This isn't cruel — it is consequential.

There are circles of
sober alcoholics he
can join to gain the
communication and the
knowledge of recovery.

I understand them because I am one
And did get sober many years ago
What alcoholics do is what I've done
There are meetings and steps to undergo
Self-loathing isn't a permanent state
I've earned my freedom and my confidence
I learned how to pray and to meditate
And uncover the snares of consciousness
The hopeless desperation is a gift
A metamorphosis is possible
To perceive differently is a lift
To balance emotion is plausible
I don't live at all like I did before
And am not self-destructive anymore.

Thoughts and emotions
need not be weightier than
the clouds in the sky
if I can let go of them
then that is liberation.

The distant horizon is salmon pink
I have always loved watching the sunrise
Something about it forces me to think
It's more than a festival for my eyes
The trees are beautiful black silhouettes
Making a worthy foreground for the sky
There is a magic that we all possess
The power of consciousness in disguise
Intellect and emotions coalesce
Sensuous exploration clarifies
In meditation being may fluoresce
Disruptive circumstances harmonize
As the uprising sun may crystallize
There is a depth in peace to realize.

The moon is on
a different angle than
the spinning earth
as the moon shines before dawn
and after the sun rises.

I want to play and be spontaneous
I'm not aiming to be nasty or lie
I'd like to winnow what's extraneous
To empower me to hit the bullseye
My topics are contemporaneous
Some people are angry but I stand by
All kerfuffle is simultaneous
So many grievances do multiply
And opinions are miscellaneous
I am only an ordinary guy
But the sunrise is momentaneous
I'm not sure I'm making sense — but I try
And it is worthy to be conscientious
I'm not sure it's possible — I can't lie.

Dr. Seuss wrote children's books
He wrote funny rhyming hooks
Thing One and Thing Two
They matter to you
We all love his storybooks.

The trick in life is to be lovable
The trap to avoid is rigidity
Love is happiness love is flammable
It consumes the heart with rapidity
It's most helpful to be adaptable
Be like water possess fluidity
No one's perfect we all are fallible
To condemn yourself is stupidity
And to make mistakes is acceptable
Meditation offers lucidity
So much of the world can be magical
Be enlightened with pellucidity
There's more to life than being logical
Find wisdom in the mythological.

I start my day with my cat
And every morning we chat
We wrestle and fight
And he tries to bite
We have a playful combat.

I don't want to be ceremonial
I'd like to think I have sincerity
I favor words that are colloquial
Without descending to vulgarity
It's not hard to be sanctimonial
With a scornful familiarity
But it's more playful to be jovial
Being deceitful is barbarity
To utter jargon would be provincial
I want joyful conviviality
The meaning should be unmistakable
A lightning bolt comes from temerity
With an added touch of hilarity.

God help me I'm liking it
Looking for the rhymes that fit
I sit on my butt
And create rut
Being a silly nitwit.

The patter of words is delectable
And the lines are a pleasure to compose
The easier words are more digestible
And then they may topple like dominoes
Sometimes my manner is questionable
Being mischievous I won't foreclose
A sly subtlety is detectable
As every new line will superimpose
It is horrid to be predictable
I keep in my pocket a yellow rose
Oh my habits are uncorrectable
I am a rascal right down to my toes
I am trying to be respectable
But the rhyming is too obsessional.

So often I am doing it
Can't really excuse it
It's a waste of time
Just trying to rhyme
Pretty soon I will stop it.

Each of my poems is a flirtation
In a way I'm saying "come play with me"
You don't have to — there's no obligation
But playing with words is my specialty
You don't need crafty sophistication
Poetry can be light and feathery
I don't harbor any expectations
But how many ways can we say "Whoopee"?
I won't pronounce fussy declarations
I won't be a scary mournful banshee
Having fun needs no justification
We can frolic like golden bumblebees
The words are more than mere decoration
They may inspire your liberation.

Let's try for simplicity
With happy complicity
We don't need bother
We won't use blather
We can have felicity.

The air is alive with the presence and
The songs of birds again in the light of
The rising sun at Pioneer Park as
I see an orange tanager in the

Oak and hear the irrepressible cheers
Of house finches and a squadron of geese
And of trumpeter swans make their arrow
Formations in the sky and the crows are

Busy communicating while flying
Continuously between the trees and
I see a crow carrying twigs in its
Beak as drops of melting snow are falling

Steadily from the eaves of the wooden
Shelter making spring music on concrete.

We group of happy
ex-drunks gather in the park
conversing about
sobriety while bingeing
on spring optimism.

It's common among problem drinkers to
Worry after having a dream wherein
The aspirant for sobriety has
Failed and given in to temptation and

Is stupefied drunk again and burdened
With a dump-truck load of shame and saddened
With the perplexity of whether to
Honestly admit his relapse to his

Faithful companions or to make the lapse
A secret and silently carry the
Guilt but upon awakening relief
Is palpable as the experience

Was only a nighttime fantasy and
Grateful redemption arrives with the sun.

A drinking dream is
a propitious sign of
earnest effort as
it only occurs when the
drunk has determinedly quit.

It's also common among us problem
Drinkers amidst our inebriation
To squirrel away hidden bottles of
Booze in propitious places above

Door frames or in our attics and basements
Or in a thousand other sly spaces
Escaping the notice of a spouse and
After the threshold of sobriety

Is crossed many containers of liquid
Joy are forgotten like landmines waiting
For discovery and I knew a guy
Who put in fences and he littered the

Countryside with hidden bottles inside
Of culverts underneath the lonely roads.

Drunken fools
really are similar
to squirrels
hiding
acorns.

It's difficult now and I don't know why
I'm much more frantic than I want to be
There is frustration but I will get by
Usually I have more energy
That is not true and I'd rather not lie
I am just not seizing my synergy
I've become an inarticulate guy
And not the poet that I'd like to be
My mind is awake but it won't comply
If the words don't flow then I'm not happy
I will calm myself and detoxify
And God keep me from becoming sloppy
I really have to try and simplify
It is my only chance to clarify.

Morning is my apogee
Morning is my jubilee
I rise with the sun
And then I have fun
Morning is my energy.

You don't have the time to fritter away
Don't allow cogitation to stultify
You must gather yourself and seize the day
You can't let your synapses ossify
The world's a festival — go out and play
Don't let your knees and elbows calcify
You may still vacation in Paraguay
Think of all the whimsy to gratify
Excite your companions host a soirée
Contact an old friend and reunify
You might even be a little risqué
You can't let epiphanies pass you by
Liberate anxiety with reggae
Enjoy Hemingway with café au lait.

Don't be sorry don't be blue
Get over that stomach flu
Life is savory
It's not slavery
Take a trip to Katmandu.

You are lucky you aren't a crustacean
Excuse me I don't mean to speechify
You need not listen to my dictation
Being human — what does that signify?
I say it's a cause for celebration
We have both arms and legs — do you know why?
I really enjoy my ambulation
And wouldn't want to be a tsetse fly
That would be such a humiliation
I can do subtractions and multiply
And contribute to civilization
I can classify and personify
Having fingers for manipulation
And a big brain for specification.

Doggerel isn't easy
As it needs to be breezy
It has to be fun
And turn on a pun
Even if it is cheesy.

The air isn't cold but is quite chilly
The overcast sky is a gloomy gray
But I am happy and even silly
I'm pretty sure it's going to rain all day
The snow is mostly gone and there's the grass
The frost is leaving and the soil is moist
Sure it's messy now but the rain will pass
Every year at this time I do rejoice
This is different than a winter day
The air is very damp and quite misty
The dry lip-splitting air has passed away
This kind of air makes metal things rusty
I know there will be snowy days to come
But now I see no reason to be glum.

The tumultuous
howling wind of the last few
days must have roused the
roots of the trees from slumber
to take minerals again.

I confess to a little negligence
I am supposed to be reading the news
But it's an insult to intelligence
And every day it's just a nasty ooze
It's full of opinion that I don't trust
Reporters are condescending and smug
Topics they cover are meant to disgust
But the overall impact makes me shrug
I'm sure the news is manipulative
News people present slanted opinions
They think their views are authoritative
They want to foist important decisions
Reading the news is a predicament
I take it in selective increments.

I like writing poetry
It's like psychotherapy
I do not scowl
I do not growl
Usually I'm happy.

I learn a lot from my metal dumbbell
It just lies on the floor so patiently
But it has the oomph to make me humble
And I can't lift it with complacency
As it weighs exactly 100 pounds
It takes my focus and it makes me strain
And I do struggle with the ups and downs
And the effort even squeezes my brain
I do have a fear of letting it go
Because my wrists aren't quite sturdy enough
I am terrified of smashing a toe
But absolutely I'm not giving up
Usually it's a hunk of metal
But its latent force is elemental.

It's not lovely it's not art
Doesn't really warm my heart
And my dumbbell
Doesn't ever smell
Though it often makes me fart.

To any amount determinable
Without any perception deleted
Even though perhaps unmanageable
Maybe so unusually gifted
Not excluding many obtrusive things
Including the imperceptibly small
Involving the physics theories of strings
Wanting it too much creates a pitfall
Sometimes an unavoidable nuisance
Resonating in a temple bell's gong
Encompassing desperate truculence
Also the unjustifiably wrong
You see enlightenment is everything
In partnership with a pregnant nothing.

It's not me who is
responsible for this
poem as I laid
my head upon my pillow
and words came from somewhere else.

Suddenly
gloom
intensifies
with
impending
rain.

—*Tekkan*

www.ingramcontent.com/pod-product-compliance
Lightning Source LLC
Chambersburg PA
CBHW040421100526
44589CB00021B/2781